ETHEREAL

BY: PHIL CHIARA

ETHEREAL

By: Phil Chiara

Acknowledgements:
For my relentlessly supportive father, family, and the brothers and sisters I've had the pleasure of walking and crossing paths with on this road of life.

Preface

What you have before you,
Is more than just a piece of literature.
It is more than the sum of frustration and ink
With a tree's lending hand.
It is more than a compilation of a madman's passion
Exhibited through poetry.
This which you hold,
With the warmth of your touch,
Awakens,
Is a living thought.
An example of liberation.
A demonstration of how one,
Can truly unshackle oneself,
From one's inner bindings,
As well as one's environment,
And become:
One.
However, the road to self-discovery
Is a vast and foggy one indeed,
That can often lead you to mistrust and cynicism.
I don't claim to know anything in its entirety,
This is to say, this is far from a self-help,
Inspirational,
Collection of poetry,
But can more honestly be described,
As a written portrayal.
Of a man staring into mirrors,
And yelling out windows.

Foreground on the author:

I was born with the name Philip Chiaramonte. However, if you turn your attention to the cover, you'll notice this is not the name of the author. It was explained to me many times by my father and grandfather that our last name means "clear mountain," and the word "Philip," is often translated to "lover of horses"…

I lived in the fog of youth and upbringing, as most do, with the name carried boldly and blindly across my heart. Giving it no second thought. "Well, there's no changing what already is," I must have said. However, as time went on, the clouds of conditioning began to dissipate. I realized that my true-self, the characteristics of my unchangeable eternal identity, no longer fit the priorities of my youth, nor my birth-name. That is to say, they lost their relevance.

The objects of my focus at the time: playing sports, aimlessly hanging out, trying to impress people, staring at screens, feeling sorry for myself, were the products of pride and unbalanced values, but more generally, figments of the senses. An attachment to things, no one can hold on to. They were in no way related to my life's fulfillment based on what I know of myself, and that which I still envision to accomplish.

I came to the conclusion that I have to accept life as it is, for you cannot change the past. On the other hand, I have great love and respect for my family. Therefore, I merely adjusted my name to suit my spirit: "Phil Chiara" (love of clarity). Trying to never lose the noble essence of my family name that generations before me struggled to maintain, but also to lead people to a better understanding of what I value in life. I would also hope that others will come to appreciate clarity as a virtue.

This is only said given how much I understand myself at the moment of my first published compilation, but as I'll try to display, no one really gets to fully know oneself.

There's no limit to growth.

That the search within,

The excavation of ego.
However vast, unpredictable or unassuring–
Is the true path of life.
Understanding each other; the path of light.
And only in the search of soul and truth,
May you find satisfaction.
But as many strange stories go,
It begins,
In the morning glow.
When All you can make out is…

Your shadow,
          Is all that
                    Protects me from the sun.
The mountain,
          Now,
                    My angel.
My footprints in the marshland
                    Will be my lone,
                              Road map home.
It seems that
          My own weight
                    Has become my handicap.
"What lies behind you?"
          I ask,
                    As if expecting a response.

          If I could ever speak so loud…

I close my eyes,
          And hear my heart beat in tempo
                    With the call of birds overhead.

          They must be going my way…

The sun says its farewell,
          And you now glow
          With a warm aura of emotion.
I can't expect Gaia
                    To feel for me.
However,
          I can certainly feel
                    Her influence.

As if she's humming,
                    Calling for harmony.
There are whispers in the wind,
                    Vibrations in the breeze.
        A soft symphony
                    Behind what seems so obvious.
At your feet,
        Your face is but a silhouette
                    Before the setting sun.
            "What lies beyond you?"
                        I ask again.

    Somehow,
        I feel like my question was answered.
So I walk up to you
        Wanting nothing but an embrace.
                        To feel you in return.
With such beauty,
        I feel like you have
                Given me something back.
        Or that I am somehow repaying you.
I climb straight up to your face,
            And rest on your crown.
                    I look around,
                    To notice,
                        I left no trail.

    From here,
            It seems like there is no direction.
There is no way down.
                No past, no forward.
                Just the peak,
                And the now.
I realize here,
        There is no other side.

There is only a pinnacle.
A point where sides meet.
Where all is seen,
But nothing tangible.
That all can be experienced in theory.
Enshrouded in such wonder,
I ask myself:
"Where from here?"
After all, there's nothing but down.
I look straight out,
And I realize,
There are other peaks
In the distance.
And she whispers:
"There are other lives to live."

Try to make Yourself
A conduit, for souls, who
Crave that moment passed.

<u>Writing.</u>

Man's invention to conquer, if not create, time. In truth, the only means of history is through language and documentation. My belief is that the most effective way of prolonging self is through introspection and writing. The easiest way to leave something behind, is to create it. To put something of gravity into the world that was not previously there.

It helps in expression of emotion, thought, and spirit. In seeing things for what they are. Not just to a fine detail, but also with a depth that resonates with who you are. Creating something timeless in the process. Everyone has their medium, whether it be music by some means, physical art, dance, acting, etc. In my opinion, writing is the most efficient and thorough method of reflection and in turn self-development.

I'm of the belief that the better someone gets at being aware and attentive of their surroundings, getting into the "mind of a writer/artist," the easier one can express themselves and better assess situations in life. Meaning, One looks at the world in a way, searching for the beauty in life, as if to capture it. On the other side of that, to an extent, reading about another's experiences, helps One prepare for the same instances if they should ever end up having to cross the same river.

I say this, not in hopes that you'll dash away to begin writing the story of your life, but that you adapt on how I came to such a conclusion, and that you find your own solution. For true education is not in explaining how it's done, but in teaching the person to learn on their own. For you can walk up to a raging river, your obstacle, and go about it exactly how you were instructed to cross it, and still be swept out. Not, however, if you adapted on that lesson learned, to fit the situation. To move past the great obstacles in life takes practice, trial and error, intuition, and allowing assistance. Certainly not by having a fixed viewpoint, going against the flow.

Within these pages, are the thoughts that strangle the mind of a young poet in a world that's trying so hard to stray from the truth. There is so much beneath the surface that begs to be brought to light. There's so much corruption, starvation, depression, all from misleading information. I'm a strong believer that in order to change the world for the better, we must first better ourselves, and our understanding of it. My goal is not intentionally to influence, but to enhance. I aspire to see more thinking about and appreciation for lasting novelties. Therefore, I'd like to try to tie spirituality and science together with a little logic, to sift out the unified truth from the subjective falsities.

Please keep in mind, this is a compilation of work from over many years. It has been written by the same person, but from many different viewpoints. It is not a how-to or a self-help book (though, feel free to use it as such) as much as an introspective exposé . I would just ask that you, the reader, to look at each poem within its own frame. That each on its own is a painted picture. Every word, like a brush-stroke, was for an intended purpose. However, there's always…

The Futility in Writing.
Nothing is ever completed.
Something is cashing in
On your borrowed time.
Every moment on the page,
Is the past
Overtaking the present.
A bookmark,
Crazed pause.
It's not like one can ignore her
When Inspiration taps you on the shoulder.
You don't tell her to wait;
Hold on till you're a little older.
You grit your teeth and listen.
Be grateful for her interest.
Some people,
She'll never reach.
Many treat her so badly,
Even abuse her.
Be joyful of her trust in you.
Take her often-pestering presence,
As a divine compliment.
Her cries of attention,
Terms of endearment.
When I lie to sleep,
She shakes me to remember.
As the ink dries to the page,
She whispers for more.
I give her my hand,
And true emotion.
She's then the one to
Move my hand.
One thing I can never do,

Is ask her to go.
At times…quite often…
She's my only company.
And it pains me
When I have to go off looking.
Inspiration may be my affliction,
Who relentlessly invades my sleep,
Prevents me from stopping,
…When she's gone,
I'm but a man scribbling to myself…
I rely on her.
I hope others may appreciate
My blight.
That someone may see her as I do,
Through the words she lends me.
The lonely poet,
But a burdened puppet.

Quite often, I feel I am gifted poems and many lines. Where at times it seems other forces take the reigns. Countless instances since childhood I would feel a thought wash over me, and consume the present moment. I would stop walking in my path, or scribble on my hand to make sure I always got down what popped into my head that registered as "right-on." I thought when I was trying to get in touch with said force of creation, I would feel as though I was fishing into the air above/behind my head and that something up there would swoop in and guide my pen, as if possessed by lines of poetry. This, I call the Ether.

It would evoke such a feeling of rightness, such a euphoric understanding, that it was meant to be. That in a way, at that very moment in time, it was exactly what I needed to be doing to fulfill my fate. Writing that line. Giving that person that info or gift. That by doing anything else, or a moment in the flow forgotten, would have been off course. I'm sure people recording a good guitar riff or splattering paint across a canvas, get the same satisfaction if they believe that to be true.

Over time, the feeling of a line popping into my head faded away and was replaced with a state of mind. In my current belief, I attribute this to the fact that I was in a meditative mentality; a state of heightened awareness. That which I label the "Ether" is more a unified field of consciousness. A point in which your memories contain experiences outside of your own. Your genetic instincts co-working with divine understanding.

In the end, it may not be the air above my head that I thought of as a child, but neurologically emitted/stimulating waves that we are all attuned to, and affected by, on a non-sensory level, along with the influence of the memory stored in our DNA. I believe those factors combined allow yourself to be a receiver for the emotions in the air, and/or even passing spirits who crave that current experience, allow you to see yourself in other forms you otherwise wouldn't.

To better understand ourselves, we must see ourselves not just in our several physical forms, but also in its multiple etheric forms. All in an attempt to bring our self-image to a singularity. However, with so many factors and variables, the search for your eternal identity seems as endless as existance itself. In that, we can often find guidance in beings existing in dimensions mostly outside of our ability to sense and comprehend. Such as spirits, which exist in a realm outside of our normal perception.

For instance, we can only perceive a small percentage of the light spectrum and although there is no space between atoms they are an almost massless energy field. So what is there to disprove the Native American belief that the empty space we deem "air," which would be empty with or without oxygen, is not in fact occupied by spirits? Also, what is there to disprove the use of yoga and shamanism to strengthen the connection between the physical mind, to the higher mind?
Or the other layers,
      Telling us,
           So that others may appreciate,
                  The beauty often unseen.

I'm sitting at the end of the world.

The very edge!

At least, where it ends in my eyes.

A pier on the Pacific coast.

The boats fishing offshore

In the new-moon void.

They shine lights,

Like day,

Out to sea,

And it looks to me,

Like a bubble.

A luminescent pearl of light,

And the night, my oyster.

I look to my sides to see

The black sand beaches,

Which made the crashing waves

Look like they were yo-yoing

Off the ledge of shore.

I swear I didn't breathe for an hour

In the awe of it.

Certainly a memory I wish to keep.

Well, I grew up in the east of Boston, Mass.,

As east as east goes,

Without crossing over.

On my last day home,

I spent it on the harbor

Looking out at the Atlantic and

Its endless dirty water.

Taking in the sharp, salty, east coast air,

One homesick sigh at a time.

So here I am:

Venice, California.

                    I breathe the same, but the air,
          A little thicker, congested,
                              And my reasons more descript.
I sit here and realize:
          You always crave home.
                    Not that home's a place,
                              But, you're constantly searching
                                        For a place to rest.
                    A place to feel welcome
                              In your own skin.
Now,
     Looking into emptiness,
                    With common reality to my back,
                              I realize the road isn't much different.
Releasing yourself to the mystery before you,
                    While relinquishing the past.
Know that nothing behind you,
                    Changes how far you can see.
It's just constantly there
          Hinting at you,
                    That these steps,
                              Don't really feel too different.
                              That this path is more paved
                                        Than it appears.
Well,
     A wise man once told me that,
                              Life is like a racing track.
You blindly keep moving forward,
                    Almost unfazed by the
                              Changing and repeating scenery,
                                        Trying to finish your race,
But you always end up circling back
                              To where you started.

                    Most see this as where they came from.
However, here I am,
                    In a reflection of where I started my journey.
And like any mirror,
                    The scenes are inverted.
My lines,
          Though the same,
                    Are refracted and hold more gravity,
                              Now with alot more in my rearview.
However, the mystery of the road
                    Remains unchanged,
                              And the game repeats itself again.
I appear so certain,
          But doubt plagues me.
                    Who on Earth wants to
                              Erase their displacement?
There are many routes on the way,
                    Untaken,
                    And much scenery,
                              Unseen,
And it's this freedom and love
          That mean the world to me!
                    Somewhere in that's
                              The home I'm craving.
But the problem as I view it,
                    Is how we see reality.
                              Something I'm sure is an illusion.
And what anyone of authority has told me,
          Was meant to
                    Spread this contusion that is confusion.
It's just hard to run parallel,
                    To what the whole world sees as true,
And it's hard to believe that near everyone's a fool,

Rather than just you.

So why am I at least this sure?

Well,

Because the world's behind me,

With those thoughts.

And sometimes it's not knowing how to live,

But simply,

How not.

Well in this circling, spiraling,

Of my racetrack,

I've found home again.

A place where I'm comfortable in my own skin,

But I damn-well remember

What that wise man said,

And that's:

When you return home,

Well,

There's just no stopping.

So I sit here at the edge,

With everything I know

Put in the past,

And I look out at the emptiness,

And I swear,

It just laughs.

But one thing still bugs me,

And that's,

How,

So many,

Still see reality,

Like the world,

As flat.

Well I certainly,

Hand it to the sea,

That I'd rather look towards the mystery,
      Than,
            To ever look back at that.

After I graduated high school, I took what funds were saved for college, sold most of my things, and used it to move to LA to attend film school. To make a sad, long story short, I ended up losing my grant, having loads of apartment/lady troubles, and resorted to having to find a real job. For over two years I worked at a college post office (miserable…). It was quite an interesting situation and is a story to tell on its own.

However, it was a position I had no say in. I was under the impression I was going to be able to take classes along with working at the university but that program was cut to one class a semester a few months prior to me starting. I worked there for two long years. They treated me like the town's scolded scapegoat and I didn't want to bother, nor give them the satisfaction of mention. After all, it was just a roadblock in life, but also a means of inspiration. For in the end, it helped perpetuate the life I built there in LA.

The university, being quite the melting pot, also allowed me to meet a lot of amazing, different, glowing people. And no one can deny California is one of the more beautiful places on Earth. I grew a lot from from the experience. I learned a bit of true tolerance, what it was like to be part of the system, and I had time to develop my Dharma (personal belief system). Also, to do what makes yourself happy regardless of outside opinion, which is the writer's riddle.

The point being, things did not work out…at least not as planned…I had a job when many didn't, I had the the pleasure of intertwining paths with many amazing people in the process, and relieved many a worried soul. However, I felt in the conditions in which I was working, that I was being wrung of my life daily. So, what was I still doing there perpetuating the cogs of oppression? I was watching, learning, saving, and planning…but that's a story to tell far from now…In reality, I was just enjoying the times with my friends in the concrete, collagen jungle of Hollywood.

Broken dreams,
        Thoughts,
            And hearts,
                Lay on the boulevard.
Misplaced expectations
                Are trampled underfoot.
Every inch of city sidewalk
                Caked with sweat.
The bustle of bumping bodies,
                And alluring laughter,
        They drown the individual.
The flashbulbs,
        Signs,
            And streetlights,
        Oh how they shine so bright!
The sharp sirens
            Slice through traffic
                And soft ears.
The patter of plastic tires
                Clicking over the cracks
        Of the smooth star-studded sidewalks.
Hash highways
            Pinned by pockets of pennies.
The starry night
            Clouded by the crying sky.
Girls,
        Crazed by sunset.
The moon hums a mad melody.
The busking bastards beg,
Happily hoping,
            Hungry...

The slight sound of plucking strings.
The hollow exhale of melancholy harmonica.
The brutal bashing of bucket drums.
        The sullen sounds of the city.
They're enveloping,
                    Discouraging,
But homely,
                And warming.
As the sharp sirens
                Wash by,
Protecting-serving-saving,
Fishing-surfing-waiting,
Not doing much in my mind.
The madness of the masses
        Frustratingly flow forward
                Into stagnant lines around
                        Stark street corners.
People passing out flyers,
                    Cards,
                        Wristbands,
Bitter barking,
            Staggering,
                    Shaking hands.
The air filled
            With bacon-wrapped hotdogs
                        And vegetables for flavor.
On carts wheeled out every night,
                To cut out a few chunks of cheese,
                            For their own family to feed.
Teenagers teetering on the edges of tour buses,
        As parents watch with weary eyes
                Trying to defy the future society provides,
And just as quiet seems to settle,

Cars fly by,
      With whooping cries,
            Of ecstasy and crashing nights.
Heavy-headed hipsters,
Wallow over hollow walkways.
Afraid to look too long,
      For eyes might meet.
Too scared to stop,
      On the cold city street.
The puddles in the gutters
      Reflect their own confusion.
Bound but held together by the past.
      Looking at the world through fogged glass.
            Forgetting the world of trees and grass.
Idleness is our reality.
            Distraction our misery.
If you live a life of vanity,
      You'll realize how it's tawdry.
Studying evil in silence.
      What's pagan is now proof.
        Freedom is now foreign.
           Religion our roof.
Sky no longer a limit.
      Impossible but a figment.
        But we ride a horse without pigment,
           For we left our ambition timid.
      We're far from stranded souls.
      For we're all alone
      There's no place called "home"
        We were born to grow.

Living in Los Angeles and having the majority of my friends hang out in Hollywood, genuinely made me feel as though I was part of a family of orphans, scurrying between the legs of pale horses ridden by Napoleonic giants. The city of money, hierarchy, corruption, and ego; a modern-day Babylon. The people of little money, the people of no money, and the people who sort-of-but-not-really-wished-they-didn't have money, appear to be the crowd that you would run into working the floors of past fame.

The lot of us had ambitions, but…we were working on it…we would spend our time jamming out, having a few brews, a blunt or two, conversations that could kill whole afternoons, all for the sake of progression. In the hopes that by playing in houses on the hills and meeting folk in the heart of Hollywood, we would find the spark needed to blow up somewhere, somehow, as legend goes.

Through my experiences in LA and Hollyweird, one thing a good friend of mine and amazing poet often said, which has many times rung true since, is: "Hollywood is my location, not my destination. Get back on the road, son, you'll only find yourself here." I've found this to be true for any city in America, but Hollywood certainly facilitates a comfort in ignorance and to a degree all its own. There seemed to be only one way out, and that was to grow.

I'm Just a Photo Album.
Developing day by day,
Month by month,
Page by page,
Phase by phaze
By craze
By chase!
Rearrange my waking mind,
And leave the rest up to time.
The illusion of now, forever present,
The height of transcendence,
Through descent,
I,
Press myself up against my reflection,
To, see if I am two.
I honestly believe it's hard to see,
What anyone says as true.
Well, isn't that true?
Or that too?
Am I just talking in circles here?
Or do you see it all a rouge?
Do you understand how much
Concentration goes into
Making this kind of juice?
Imagine:
Everything's vibrating-brating
Shaking, empty, but awakened
Walkin' loose!
Making up our minds.
Our minds in the making.
Erasing…Erasing…
Starting it all off at the beginning,
With that lingering,

Past lives craving,
Constantly searching,
Mind in need of quenching,
A thirst unrelenting,
The open road,
The home,
For those,
Whose souls,
Need stretching,
Without constantly defending,
Like a memoir with no ending,
Or a book with no title.
And to walk a mile
In those shoes
Would certainly
Take a while!
For that's our style.
Sideways, backwards,
Wherever beauty lies.
Only the glare of the evening sun
Shielding our eyes.
Without fear,
We barrel through
The scree and debris
Covered highways.
Hitting triple digit speeds
Yelling "YAHOOEEE!!"
With no reason
Need mentioning.
Just know things
Become nature over time,
So don't do anything
You don't want to be,

                              too repetitively…
And to be free,
            In your own eyes,
                        Is all you can aspire to be.
But to think so liberally,
            People will think you crazy.
                  To live life your own way,
                        You'll never see yourself lazy.
Just gotta keep moving,
                  Never stop,
                        For time stops for nothing.
To have something
                  Worth dying for,
                        Leaves you with
                              A life worth writing.

<u>I sit cross-legged</u>
In a darkened room.
Eyes closed,
In deep thought,
As I awoke.

I thought I would be
Accustomed to the night.
That I could make out
Some definition in the shroud.
However, the glowing outline of
The doorway, caused enough contrast,
To make it the only identifiable vision.
Whatever is beyond that door,
Whether it be a single candle,
Or several suns,
Is irrelevant.
It is the strongest force
In the room.
My attention is drawn
To the irradiating keyhole.
Not of the modern variety;
Tiny, indistinguishable, in the knob,
But one made for a skeleton.
Above the knob,
And a clear gateway to whatever lies beyond.
I stand before the door.
Close enough to defrost
My cold-stricken nose,
But not enough to escape
The frivolous shadow lingering behind.
What tortures me,
Is that I know what lurks in the darkness behind me,

And I was actually quite comfortable.
                        That is,
                                Until I realized there was more.
It appears as though, beyond this door,
                        Lies a better place.
                                A place of light and warmth.
However, logical reasoning
                        May be my ruin.
I could be tricking myself,
                        And hell incarnate could be
                                Behind that door.
A new world of wonder could be waiting,
                        Or my curiosity could be controlling me.
As I ponder my next move,
                One fact stands atop the rest.
                        That though I am comfortable if I remain,
                                And secure in my destiny,
                        This will be all I ever know.
I know close to what this shroud
                Has in store for me,
                        But with the knowledge of another choice,
                I can no longer remain content.
To open the door to face death,
                Would be a risk worth taking,
                        If the alternative is constant stagnation.
And if the world on the other side
                Is anything like where I am now,
                        At least I would know of another.
So I walk up to the door.
                I go to reach for the handle
                        Through the ray of light from the keyhole,
I grasp the knob,
                Searing to the touch.

I turn it slowly,
      Enjoying the burn.

      And I awake
From deep thought.
    Eyes open,
In a bright room,
  Legs crossed.

So smooth,
        Like a highway drive.
So smooth,
        Like a summer night.
So smooth,
        Like an inner thigh.
So smooth,
        Like the morning light.

Alcohol poisoned,
      Bile stained,
            Sunday morning sidewalks.
Hollyweird-broken women ask for change
                And a place to stay,
Gowned in club-tight dresses as if any other day.
Those with nowhere else,
        Find refuge in the warm subways
        Once the cold air of night
                meets the light's ray.
I swear the sidewalks of LA
        Will be the death of me,
    If those returning from the bars don't get me first.
Acclaimed bathhouses of fallen fame,
        Gladly accept the blame,
          As if it were some game
            To tame,
               The wild ego.
But it seems they wouldn't have it any other way
Decadence,
    Their ecstatic,
        Codependent amigo.
And if you haven't already smelled it,
          You'll catch the Beirut king himself,
Mistaking a light post for a tree,
      In this jungle-like sea,
          Of unwarranted enemies.
And the man who knows nothing but,
        Apparently lost his strut,
          Along with his faith in humanity.
Good morning,
    Goes without saying,
        For it's so hard to tell if you're awake.

But it's a new day,
So I guess you can be grateful
You're still part of this illusion in some way.

Brush your shoes off,
        Leave your mask by the door,
Because
        I'm looking for who you are,
Not someone I knew before.

Well...there's something very mystic about Hollywood...some form and flow of an attractive, creative energy; controlled, distorted, if not just misdirected. There are many people who would claim that Osiris's phallus is buried in the hills and its energy is being manipulated through "free masonry." That the city was in fact built to be the hub of Western culture, and to have said phallus as close to Mt.Shasta (considered the root Chakra of Earth) to cause Pranic and Apanic miscommunication.

Apana in Sanskrit means "downwards air," and Prana translates to "air of life" or the energy of Source. To have the most grounding and humbling energy point on Earth, with the source of creativity in Egyptian lore above, paved over with buildings and temples to alter its impression and context. Also a horde of cloudy-headed, conditioned tourists, corruption, and confusion running over it........I wouldn't stake my reputation on this claim, but it certainly explains more than I'd like to go into detail about in script. I still very much value my life to annoy anyone with sufficient resources.

The problem, regardless of cause, is that we forget we exist. For one to acknowledge his or her own existance, they need to be focused on the now. This is what yoga can aid in. To silence all thoughts of what has been done, what needs to be done, and to focus on the doing. For that is all there really is: the moment being experienced. That you are here, now, and all else is illusion. It is to see reality in its essence.

When we are focused on our existance, we are in turn drawing our focus to the balance and flow of Prana and Apana within ourselves. Prana, the energy of life from Source (the point of which all energy originates from), serpentining down your spine from your crown to your root Chakra. Apana, Maya, the illusion, the energy of the material world, rests in the lower Chakras and spirals upwards from Earth.

When we are overwhelmed by Apana, we are forgetful of our existence. Our true-selves bound not by death, but only by the cycle of reincarnation (Samsara). Therefore, once that fact's forgotten, we would be dragged back to the turmoils of the material world and burden of our physical self. Prana being of a pure and transcendental quality, consumes all and clarifies. In the act of many forms of yoga, what you are attempting to do is use the divine flow of Prana, to overwhelm the Apanic energy that drags you back down to the forgetfulness of your eternal individualized soul. To bring you back from the illusion.

I want to also clarify that Apana is not negative in nature, though the adverse of Prana, something positive. It is just a deviation from truth. If walking on a dirt trail in the midst of tall grass, you could not rightly say that those walking alongside in the grass are going the wrong way; only that if the trail's the only means to the destination, it would seem quite pointless to trudge through the grass the majority of the way, or to wander, if you truly desire to reach the end of the trail (all based off of personal fufillment). If so, being transfixed in the unified consciousness, in a Theta mind-state, meaning to be cleansed and fueled by Prana, will put you on that path, while Apana will lead you astray.

There's plenty of research that proves that the Earth, too, not only has its own Chakra points, but also works under the same principles as the ones associated with the body. They are to be open, spinning, flowing, and allowing in both energies. However, just like in our case, they also require balance, or they will be brought back to the imperfect, unhappy physical existence.

In this hypothesis, the situation with Southern California, and more specifically, greater Los Angeles is that it was an area built to be the center of Western culture, predestined to be the focal point of creative minds and energies the world over. It was to house the Egyptian allegorical equvilant of the source of all art and creation atop the Earth's root Chakra so that for whatever reason, when we go to such a city to look for fufillment and our true calling, associating ourselves with our physical identity, we find a very humbling energy influencing our higher self. This leaves the physical mostly unaware of the source of such emotions for it does not come from something comprehended by the senses.

This is also the reason why people are generally more active at night. It is because there is less active external stimuli, or at least less hectic, interfering with your own. Even more prevalent when One is isolated.

However, please understand, you can never create more energy by yourself than you can with others who understand.

Your true-self, being of transcendental nature, is acutely affected by such influence. When it expects the humbling and grounding effects of Earth's root Chakra, while being diluted by the effects of a materialistic and egotistic populace, a selfish, degrading system, and energy of a much polar nature, you can tell that it is quite a struggle to sift through such influences to say the least. If we let such material factors effect our physical self, it leaves us quite unfulfilled, depressed, lost. However, when we are in acknowledgement of our existence, transfixed in the now, and aware of One's eternal individualized self, we find an exemption to the conditioning. By being focused on your true-self, you are in fact being focused on your connection with the source of all energy and creation, and are instating the purifying properties of Prana. Unfortunately, we are preset in this painful dimension of reality, and therefore, any attempt to maintain contact with your higher self will be short-lived, without much practice in self-realization and yoga.

Most of us, including myself for most of this life, are completely clueless of the meaning of half the terms I'm throwing around. However, say this in the hopes that you crave a look within. Maybe you feel yourself inspired to find your own way to the trail. For those of us who believe they already see through the illusion, a little food for thought. This appears as an observation of just one major city in one country, but the effect cannot particularly be measured and it certainly effects us all (this being one of many controlled Chakra locations). If anything, it's better to entertain a thought to deny it, than to cast it off without taking anything from it.

If there's one thing I want to make clear, it's that we are not just our physical selves, but also our undying true identity. That the personality we associate with is much more than the make up of our geneology, or what sign you are in astrology. You are a soul of thousands of incarnations. That no matter what form it takes on, it will always have some representation/resemblance of you. However, to make sure you're on that trail, and not lost, wandering among the tall grass, requires that you make the effort to acknowledge who you are identifying with. That being said, I believe that once we fix the interference within ourselves, we can then work to fix our planet's identity problem.

The Reverberation of Source
Settles in tempo with time.
It resonates through our frosted
Hearts and minds.

Bound not by thought,
But thought possible.
And the limit,
Only you define.

We are infinite luminescent love,
In need of shedding our shells.
My heart tells me this is true,
And I hope you feel it too.

That spinning, spiraling,
Holographic hole in your chest.
Calling to unleash us
From self-mindedness.

To lose who we think we are,
And return our focus back to the stars.

Our hearts now
Wink themselves to sleep.
For rest is all it remembers.

It used to be our all,
But now it follows
The mind's orders.

If we distribute our love
In the right places,
In honor of mending our mistakes,

We can build a new world,
In our unity,
And can correct our corrupted state.

There is no good or evil.
It's just a figment of duality.
A developed masculine mindset,

A habit,
That has unraveled reality.
We're all matter,
And of the same source.
No matter's destroyed,
Just returned to the Earth.
And if unfufilled,
The soul reforms,
And the stories of past lives,
Are just lessons learned.
Soon these memories
Will resurface,
Those with rusted hearts,
Reawakened.
Remember,
Nothing is instant,
Nor perfect,
But our future is now,
In the shaping.
The power of change
Is in our favor.
The world of the past
Is drifting.
And that feeling of
Fear and uncertainty,
Is just your consciousness
Shifting.
There will be a divide,
Of those who lead,
And those left behind,
And those that find,
Comfort in shadow,
Will try to challenge the light.

There will always be
         An opposing force,
                    But the truth knows no sides.
And those of right,
         With love in their hearts,
                    Will return back to the skies.
But first we should see us all as One,
                    And lose this person called "Me."
There's no sense waiting
         On God's son,
                    For Christ is all-encompassing.
We have nothing to fear but ignorance,
                    The only true foil of love.
I know we're all looking for proof,
                    So how can you ignore the abyss above?
There are supposedly 11 layers of dimensions,
                    And infinite universes within!
Even more than that, galaxies and planets.
                    So it's foolish to think this is it!
To be so focused in this realm,
         Is a waste of your purpose.
                    We're all just cells of a planetary organism,
                    Our job now to heal the surface.
So grab the flame within yourself,
         To shatter the shadow that shades.
                    Let go of the past and the future,
                    And that wasteful emotion: hate.
And if you may,
         I'd like to,
                    Leave you with something,
                              To hold on to:
There is no division,
         There is no <u>you</u>.

There is no blind faith,
         There is only <u>truth</u>.

The River of Life,
  Flows continually onward.
Emerald glowing
  Tablets of light,
    Illuminating the way
      Past words and writing.
Cremating conscious thought,
    Bridging our minds.
We must brave
    The hallowed hallways
        To reach the light!
Oh! Men of science!
        How we've lost our spirit…
            We dare not stray any further!
For He,
    Recorder of legacy and love,
        Life and light.
Will leave you lost
        In your own right.
Our origin,
    But a nostalgic dream.
        Far from our relative comprehension.
We used to live forever.
        Here,
          We only live for now.
We the people of muddled mind,
      Can only be blinded
        By our holy center.
          For we simply,
            Forgot how to see.
We are born
    The children of light,
      Fueled by eternal fire,

Destined to carry the torch of wisdom,
Through the smog it has left.
We must reawaken
The knowledge of yore,
Far within our young infinite spirits.
The answers looking for us
Are not of this realm,
But through the conduit
Of cosmic consciousness.
Between the lessons of death,
And the lessons of life,
Lies a key...
A key to be learned,
If not taught,
And only in the search of
Soul and truth
May you find satisfaction.
We have been detached,
Like roots cut from a tree,
Or coral from its reef.
We are lost afloat,
Looking for soul,
Craving the whole!

We are messengers of the sun.
Void of both remembrance,
And direction.
Though we know quite well
What we carry,
And we bear that with us
Through the darkness.
We do so with the inate understanding,
That at the end of the narrow tunnel,

There will be light,
            Waiting to embrace us.
And it's no wonder
            That we've become so lost,
We've fell for the martyrs,
            Ignoring the cost,
The sunken cities,
            The warnings of Thoth.
      For in the end, they were intentionally for not.
One thing I've learned
            From this plane
            Is to follow your heart,
                        But only if led by spirit.
For your heart
      May be swayed by the mind,
                  But the spirit always follows the light.
Well of course the truth would be
                  Hard to comprehend,
If not, we would have known it,
                  And this journey fruitless,
The fact is
            The whole time
                  it's right in front of us,
And that is,
            Nothing in life
                  Is worthless.
We will soon see
            The guiding hand,
                  And it will drag its finger
                              Across the Earth
Reawakening
            The sleeping lands,
                  And correcting

                            Our spiraling curse.

"Surely in time,
            Ye are one with the master.
Surely by right,
            Ye are one with the master.
And surely by right,
            Ye are one with the All."

And let that be
            Our rallying call!

_____

Let's just say,
     If by the end of your life,
          You wanted a boat.
               To sail the world,
                    See the seas,
But you've found yourself lodged
     In the grays and beiges of office culture.
          Scheming, saving, to one day,
               Be engulfed in earthly blues.
Well those people,
     Many times,
          Over time,
               Lose their sight,
                    As they get older.
End up blind with what they have.
     Content with what's closest to them.
          Conjure up a different dream.
               Make it seem like all their wants,
                    Are all their needs.
To fall short of a dream,
     Is a travesty.
          Never relinquish the reigns,
          Of your destiny.
               Why not trade your desk and office,
                  For a job on the sea?
Pivot thy path right there!
     Avoid the current of distracted sheep,
               And grow straight to your goal!
Make your life
     Worth its while.
          Don't let fear and uncertainty
         Prevent you from
           Getting through.

It's up to you to choose.

For life gives
  To those who ask,
    And search for truth,
      Just that.
        In abundance.

If you give into fear,
  Fate will make you face it,
But if you give it hope,
  It will return to you every reason to be.
Don't hesitate to reach for your dreams,
    They're closer than you think.
Stay positive for what you desire,
   For excuses are your only obstacles.

There's a change in motion,
A flux in the breeze.
The autumn has fallen
From the August leaves.
The rivers rush rampant,
Washing away the banks.
Erasing, resetting,
Destroying all ranks.
Rebuilding and reforming,
Starting anew.
It's destined
It's for this generation to do.
And whether or not,
We admit that it's true,
Things just go the way that
They intend to.
These words reel out of me
And it's strange to say:
I'm not the person standing
Before you today.
An illusion, a figment,
But a reflection of a pigment.
We're all just light
Reformed in a way.
So the person before you,
The person you see,
Is a reflection of yourself,
That is me…
Now that we're all on a level plane,
We can look at each other,
And acknowledge we're the same.
We can both go our own separate ways,
And know, in no way,

Did we really change,
Only bring us back to
What's more natural,
And to lose the intent to
Be so empirical.
And to think such a radical change,
Can be so simple,
And it only just takes a step!
So here at the forefront,
We relinquish what's store-bought,
And take to arms,
With passion in hand.
Realizing we're all kindred souls,
Intent to only bring warmth to the land,
And our fellow man.

The Open Air

Expressed with an exhale
A breeze
A gust
A sneeze
A vast field of fallen leaves
A view void of trees
A place to breathe
A place to be, without being seen
A place of release
Free
Root
A place to grow
A place to grow, without being shown
Fertile soil under snow
Dead earth above
Life brewing below
The rock
The flow
The solid ground is
All we know

Scrounging the Earth to know her better.
Looking for clover in the flowers.
The grass lies flat,
From scavengers of the past.

I feel like if given so many,
To give them away,
For nothing green ever lasts,
And we all shrivel so fast.

An artificial miracle.
The relation so simple.
But something in the search,
Is what gives it worth.

Something in the wonder,
Of careless generosity.
Like a memory's birth,
In relation to the Earth.

I look up and ask for guidance,
As if ignorance met innocence.
The end's all that I meant,
With all this meaning spent.

No shade on this road,
        No one was ever told,
                How in the end, life is only lent.

In my short lifetime thus far, I've had the pleasure of finding quite a few four-leaf clovers. I've found them on breaks at work, the outfields of little league games, my own backyard, and almost anywhere there was grass. However, they weren't always so prevelent in my life. It all started with one Mother's Day back in elementary school.

I remember the morning clearly. I had readied myself for school and my mother was pretty disappointed that I didn't have anything ready for the occasion. I was fairly young and had no idea what day it was, but she might have also just been upset from having to wake up and drive me that morning. However, I wanted nothing more than to find a way to alleviate the tension.

The whole ride to school was a stressful one. When we eventually arrived at the gravel-laced parking lot, I opened the door and looked down to see a small patch of green in the grays with one perfect four-leafed beauty sticking out through the shamrocks (those with three leaves). Glowing in its green glory, reflecting the light of morning. I ran around the car and showed it to her eagerly, asking whether or not it was lucky. Doubting that it could possibly be true. Needless to say, it was just the surprise my mother needed that morning.

When I started finding a copious amount, I took it as a sign that I should start giving them away. For there's no better way to prove to someone that they're out there, than to satisfy the skeptical eye. I've had plenty of time to ponder the matter and I've found clovers to be a psychological wonder. The fact that they're so abundant but seen as so rare, is a grand example of how we have been conditioned to think. Or maybe they are and I'm just performing miracles…Just makes you curious, what else you just assume to be true from common knowledge…That you take such an assumption as fact and never strive for such horizons under the impression of the impossible.

Truly the concept of a miracle is a subjective one. That to believe miracles to exist at all is to say that all life and existence is miraculous. To say a person who goes years without food or water is performing a miracle, when the conditions of life on Earth harbors such sustainability, is contradictory. It is simply that we don't understand the method, that we see it as miraculous. That if a plant or animal can live in reason-defying conditions, so can we humans, if we decipher the method. In the end, if any can, we all have the ability to.

Everything is in fact a miracle, based on our perception of what is normal and what could be considered as anomalous. Therefore, in the eye of an infant that has yet to entirely personalize his or her surroundings, it sees everything from a peek-a-boo to the rising sun as a miracle. That is to say, that once the baby has played enough games of peek-a-boo, and witnessed enough sunrises, it no longer sees its wonder...or it loses its value in a sense.

The most interesting facet of clovers is that we don't know whether they are a mutation or an adaptation! This is so fascinating due to the fact that they could either be the one who wanted growth the most out of the patch, and gave everything to grow that extra leaf, consistently striving towards the sun to grasp just that much more sunlight. Or it could be a genetic super-shamrock, where one in every so many happens to be the lucky one. Either way, they are a reflection of ourselves, and that only makes itself even more apparent in the context of all the species on Earth.

Not only are four-leaf clovers proof of miracles, they are also proof that all things open your eyes to the enchantment of everyday life. They are a reflection of the Earth and ourselves. Now, to bring up all this nonsense, I would hope that you the reader may go out in search of your own. Though I wish I could give everyone I meet who strives for the light, their own, but for you to have that deep moment between yourself and the Earth, to get lost in her greens, is an experience I have yet to be able to properly put into words. The clover will find you.

Do you feel the
      Unselfish longing?
           Do you hear the bell
              Of Source ring?
                Do you feel as
                   One with
                      Everything?
              Do you feel the love?
Legs crossed
      Across continents.
           Our unified love theory.
Surely no mystery at all,
          If one's listening.
Acceptance:
      The fiery pit before
              The crystalline ascending staircase.
You are always happy underneath,
           But often hidden,
           Behind the silkscreen of experience.
There's just so much that chance,
           Can do to a man,
                That can
                   Turn his gaze cold.
But just as sand,
      Falls from your hands.
              There's very little in this life
                   You can hold.
Compels you to turn a shoulder.
           Makes you wish you were young.
        Maybe not young,
           But to a place deemed home.
                A place that's warm.
A place you can go,

When you feel alone.
A place, encased,
In a cage of bone.
That place you seek's within, not without.
Your body,
Your temple.
Your mind,
A sanctuary.
Peace,
But a state of mind,
Hidden in the glow
Behind your eyes.
Those on the street,
Looking for a sign,
Will succumb to disappointment eventually.
For they themselves,
Are all they'll find.
If you can touch the Earth,
You can feel the divine.
May Gaia be your only crutch,
And let the sky guide.
Therein lies our unity.
Which in turn,
Reveals our frailty.
Also, where along
We lost our way,
But the truth,
Like light,
Never fades.
And even more so,
In the glow
Of a new day.
Now in the dawn, we reawaken,

From our conscious coma.
Shaken from our sullen slumber,
By the shining soma.
And as a result
From the embers
Of knowledge and love,
We can piece together
Human past
By looking from above.
Just remember:
We are All,
And all of us are one.
We are stardust,
Made of Source,
Just one of many burning suns.

Dark waves, foreboding skies,
                    Pushing lifeless bodies aside.
Frustrated lands,
             Unleashing torment.
                    Gaia's remains,
                                  Passing judgement.
                         ...
The end may be by our hands,
                    Where even the sands,
Will quiver at the thought
                    Of burning land.
                                  The end may be in our hands.
                         ...
We line the ocean with plastic,
             And wonder why we fall victim to angry seas.
                    Our planet, but a mind in herself,
                    A force that does as she pleases.
                         ...
The waters that once gave us birth
                    Will return what remains to the Earth.
                         ...
And as much as you may grimace
                    At all the cynics,
                    The witnesses
                    Tend to be more specific.
                                  The scope's just too large,
                                         To be so focused.
                         ...
Seems the end of existence
                    Is through aimlessness,
As much as all of this
                    Forgiveness of ignorance,
                                  Has taught us.

...
The neglectful are the locusts.

The cricket on my balcony,
                    Speaks to me.
Through his odd symphony,
                    Madness he plays.
Content with the sound
                    Of his own voice,
                         I had no choice,
                              But to hear what he had to say.

Someone must be a witness,
　　　　　　To these trials.
There's just too much coincidence,
　　　　　　To be in denial,
　　　　Of these road blocks so apparent.

They say you'll be rewarded
　　　　　　For your honesty,
But that's as easy to have faith in
　　　　　　As destiny,
　　　　For it seems not the burden, but how you bear it.

I have a strong belief that the transcendental dimensions are entwined with the one(s) we set to reality. I'm at least positive in my own experience of the seams that tie/entangle other dimensions with ours. There is no doubt that there are "glitches" of sorts. Such as a scientist having an effect on an experiment by just observing it. Happenings of a nature that defy the rules of the rational mind.

However, such rules are the reasons for our near-sightedness. They inhibit our ability to understand the significance by creating limits. Such as a spirit trying to interact with one in this physical realm. Often what a spirit uses to get our attention is startling to us, but also just a matter of interpretation. And often done in the greatest sincerity. We have just been sensitized to the unknown where we almost fear the transcendental.

That being said, there should be some means of consciously interacting. There should be some way to enhance our frequency or develop ourselves to the point of being able to seep through the silkscreens of reality. To gain more of an ability to interact with the other layers. Perception, being our framework of reality, is all that truly divides us from the other dimensions. However, your perception is in constant flux. From your beliefs, to your mood. Though, I believe there are many ways to enhance your perception, such as: learning about the world around you, those unseen; silencing the static of the mind; developing your skills at something; learning something new; having philosophical thoughts, as well as engaging in deep conversation.

Similar to miracles, which are often mistaken as real (though just the inability to comprehend the process, or see it from the perspective of the person performing), the concept of coincidence is just as dilutable, but less subjective. We are always told: "There's no such thing as coincidence." That we shouldn't look too much into things, for there's no point. I believe there's a reason for such a common thought pattern, but I digress. The fact is, coincidences are very real, and are keys to understanding our connection to the world around us.

A good example of this are total solar eclipses. They occur very infrequently, are recorded by civilizations around the world, can be anticipated, and are important to understanding other factors of physics by reference. For example, total solar eclipses only occur because the Sun, whose diameter is 400 times that of the moon, is coincidentally 400 times as far away from the Earth. Therefore, if the Moon were to orbit just a little further out, or were just a little smaller, they would never occur.

This all being said, my whole life I've been on the lookout for coincidences. Things that happen in sequence, playing along with the clock, a chance run-in with someone, a phone call from someone as you thought of them, meeting someone new when you were given the option to have avoided such an instance, déjà vu, foresight, etc. These appear as mere chance to someone unaware of looking deeper. The only way to interpret such instances is by filtering it through your belief system and giving it value based on your experiences.

There are many works on the subject of coincidence/synchronicity. Some theorize the ability to manipulate coincidence by learning to value it based on unified truth, to cause what could be described as, artificial miracles, or understanding the flow/layers to the point of control. I can certainly agree with the fact that coincidences are similar to a wink from God in the sense that you are given an opportunity to witness a little of nature's humor or you are being contacted by another layer of reality in some incomprehensible way. My belief is that coincidence is, in fact, you realizing the flow of nature. Like a surfer waking up in the midst of riding the inside of a barreling wave. We are looking to learn how to remain awake and not just catch glimpses of the flow we ride; to see the opportunity in the moment.

It's the seamless flow of our reality (with the new ability to know what you're looking at, i.e., seeing through/past). The individualized soul, surfing along the speeding cylindrical stream of synchronicity. It's an instantaneous breaking through of your conditioning into the collective consciousness and the divine order of our antfarm-like planet. The cosmic surfer dipping his/her hand into the curl.

I'm still far from grasping this concept and its gravity; but by paying attention to things such as reoccurring themes, circles (returning to beginning), and coincidences, I believe I have gained some bearing in my few years. I believe through these lessons that I've gained a better understanding of the true beauty in life. As a surfer in a rough swell or as a boy who learns to ride a skateboard. First, becoming one with the board and the sidewalks. Then developing control and abilities. That is, until he grows into a man who loses his dependance on it. The bird must first learn to walk, to fly, then to soar in order to realize what it has left to achieve. I've always been told to never tell someone that they are free, for it loses all meaning; but I hope in some way I got that across.

<u>The Rising Flames of the Infinite All</u>
                              Encompasses and baptizes
                                        Our childlike minds.
To breed a gust from below:
                      Prana,
                              The wind under our wings.
The young stars above
                  Look down on the chained children of man,
                                        And sigh…
Knowing they remain alone,
                  For they will never reach their realm
                              Bound by physical boundaries.
Boundaries built
              By sheer stubborn thought.
                              The cloak
                                      Of common complacence
Don't think
                  This closed-minded mindset
                                        Isn't man-made,
It is an otherworldly tool,
                  Of confusion and control,
                                        On a secular scale.

Within the Halls of Life,
                  Rooted deep within the veins of home,
                                        Grows a flower.
A flower engulfed in the cold flames of wisdom,
                  As well as doused, in the ever-expanding
                              Ocean of consciousness.
Emanating from the hallowed depths of Gaia,
                  Out to the vast openness of the Ether.
              It is knowledge incarnate.
It is the key,

To comprehending,
   This realm,
      Of reality.
By condensing spirit to
   our dimensional construct.
A fool's quest to explain,
    For it's so easy to just know!
       That:
The Flower of Life's
   Intent is to show.
To show,
  What little we actually know.
    Built on the context of the All.
That All,
  Is a whole.
   One mind,
    One soul.
Somewhere between
..............................The ellipsis of time..............................
    Sits a circle of masters.
  Wading through the aeons,
     Waiting to awake.
  Projecting their message
    To those who line the surface.
Their spirit now flows freely through
   The body of man.
Once reawakened,
  They take form.
   To guide the surface,
    Onward and upward.
  From mother to sun.
But first,
  The children of light,

Like flaring candles,
Spark up in crowds of darkness,
Like infectious balls of flame.
Igniting the paper souls
Close enough to catch on,
With intent to one day
Illuminate the world.

Such transcendence
Is not something granted,
But it certainly can be earned.
Such as love, learned,
Or the future, forewarned.
You may just be a
Flickering flame,
Ready to be kindled,
Or a wooden mountain,
Ready to be whittled,
But in the end,
We're all stuck,
Somewhere in the middle,
But our ambitions,
Shouldn't lie so low.
Our intention,
Should be to grow!
To immerse,
Ourselves in the flow,
And to relearn
What we already know.
To praise
The divine complexity,
And the intricate existence within.
The change in us,

Starts with you.
This new age
Starts from within.
So lose your "I's,"
And open wide,
To embrace a new day.
I must go,
But we'll never part so…
Namaste!

Thoughts into the distance,
                     I listen.
      Sweet whispers,
               Calling.
Telling me concealed secrets,
                  Discrete dreams.
      Telling me:
            What appears to be,
                     Isn't as it seems.

My half-past cigarette,
      A broken thought.
           Just another piece of paper,
          I must have forgot.
               Funny how the times change,
                    When they're for not.

An aged loyal friend of man,
      Limps away.
           The whimper of the melon-colored collie,
             Appears at man's feet to say
               That real love lasts,
                  Forever and a day.

They say no man,
      Can encompass an ideal.
          And no book can,
            Explain how you feel.
             But how can you prove,
               The impossible to be real?

Have you ever at any point of your life, glared at a blazing fire, stared at the endless void of night, been alone, enshrouded in the shell of evening forests for as far as you could see, and felt…nostalgic? That you haven't just seen this fire before, that this is something firmly engraved into your instincts from time immemorial. That somehow…just maybe…you were familiar with those stars before you were your own reflection, countless lives before this?

In my belief, we as a species first began to associate our surroundings with the four major elements: earth, wind, fire, water. From there we began to categorize everything relative to those precedents. Well, this goes back to what was mentioned about the stringing along of familiarities and coincidences and how they can be used as a rudder along the seas of reality. By acknowledging the basic forces of nature, you can see that everything, to its finest detail, falls along a balance of cause and effect; an equilibrium.

That being said, by realizing the string which relates instinct and emotion, could One call upon those ancient memories? Possibly get in touch with the timeless stream of knowledge, i.e., Akashic records? Well, in the author's personal experience and countless other testimonials the world over, that through meditative discipline, this is.

You are not just the result of your material genealogy but also the transgressions of your spirit's past lives. You are not just the instinctual memories of your species' development, but also the Karma carried from your former incarnations. And through the understanding of how South American shamans use hallucinogenics to understand plants and the land they inhabit, it leads us to the understanding that our DNA carries the memory/knowledge of not just our genetics, but also that of an external connection.

I see no coincidence when I gaze upon a bonfire or even the ember of my cigarette, and feel like I've had this rooted connection to the elements through my true-self for aeons in different forms. It's not by accident that the ripple in your coffee casts you off into a daydream, or that every time you look at those stars…it almost makes you homesick. My theory is that the karmic memory of your individualized identity, in conjunction with the memory stored in your DNA, determines your instinctual habits and preconceptions based off your present life's experiences, and that is what evokes the sensation of nostalgia.

Solitude,
    Retains a peaceful mind,
        Much like a picture frame
            Displaying time.
  White noise.
      A white feeling.
         I feel nothing.
Acid-wash my life away.
        Leave nothing but shades of gray,
Broken down past resolve.
      Past consolation.
         No emotions remain.
           No pain.
In this self-inflicted
    Mental purgatory,
      I take a stroll
        Through this labyrinth
          Of my own design.
Demeanor shattered,
    And goals erased.
All movement
   Stops in this place.
      Senses consumed,
        Though it leaves a bad taste.

No sense of direction.
     Up or down
      The white noise
        Cancels out all sound.
Meditation won't bring me back.
     It pulls me further into the void.
   Reality becomes
     My personal toy.

Aware of my surroundings,
         More than aware,
                  But nothing's there.
This is my world to create.
                          Thoughts in midair.
I can now control my own
         Wilderness of wonder.
                  Once neutral,
                           Now my canvas.
                                   A world of purity appears.
                                           Vast skies and clean air.
An onyx castle in the distance,
                  The center of my utopian world.
But the city so far away,
         As I sit atop the caps of the ancients,
                  Looking out into the endless emptiness.
So isolated.

I have anything I can dream.
         However, my perfect world shatters,
                  And I fade back to
                           The pains of reality.

Have I awoken? Simply gone back to sleep?
         Surely despair thrives in minds that are weak…

I'm tapping into something
          I can't comprehend yet,
                    But I love it.
A long conversation
          Of no words spoken.
What lovely, ecstatic influence.
                    Such sincere cynical innocence.
  I hope we find the communal consciousness,
          In all of us.

In a state,
    <u>Of bottomless thought,</u>
        There's a shop.
That displays great artifacts
       Of life to me.
It explains many things
      Whether or not
         You intend to buy,
    But you can give all thoughts a try.
My shop has a beige hue,
     Quite indifferent,
       Takes you places,
         You in the past visited.
And though you may not remember
    These paths you've once walked,
     These strange people you've met,
       You've many times before talked.
This is one of many windows
    I like to look through,
      Getting to know myself
        here in this state.
   I've learned:
    In love and memories,
       Lies wealth.

I was caught
  Pulling the reigns,
    While laughed at,
      By both sides of the coin.
I thought my burden
    Could be carried more swiftly,
As it is, only pride is left
      To pull my sledge.
What I trusted was
    Proven to be illusory.
So now, I'm left stranded
      On this spire
      Built of an adhesive
        Made of conscience regret.
For what I fret,
  Has all been spent,
    On one safe bet,
      That I loyally meant.
The stranger I only once met,
    Had written me back a check.
      And for the corner "for," she said:
        "For the love I'll never get back."
Held together by instincts,
    And sticks of incense.
      I admit that this is
        No time to lament.

Progression now
    My only love,
      For standing still,
        Seems so fleeting.
But just because you move forward,
      Doesn't mean you don't look back.

You're bound to repeat the past if ignorant,
        But at least what you've seen is more personal.
Advice isn't like a receipt,
        Given with purpose,
                Just to be discarded out of burden.
It's more like the change.
        Carefully counted for,
            And always an articulately crafted use.
It could be passed along
      To someone in more dire need,
        Or someone out of greater greed,
          But honor it and you'll see,
             Your advice may grow a money tree.
You reap what you sow,
      But only if you know,
          How much that receipt really means.
So watch the past,
      Make the now last,
         Or history will cease to be dreams,
             And be your nightmare…

Misery loves company,
And sleeps on the floor.
Well, I've had it and I don't
Want to live with Misery no more.

I tossed her things to the curb,
And hung my head high.
She was a weight off my shoulders.
I just waved with a sigh.

The stench of static left the air.
Nothing left holding me down,
But when my memory of her is back,
I seem to see her around town.

I saw her with a friend of mine.
He looked quite somber.
I hadn't seen a man that sad,
Since the last time I saw her.

I asked him what was wrong,
And he couldn't really recall.
He just remembers getting her number,
From the back bathroom stall.

Said she came in with a smile,
And that she wouldn't stay a while.
Gave her a blanket,
And he woke up on the kitchen tile.

No idea how he made it,
Back to the street.
But was still shackled,

With her wrapped around his feet.

But he says he loves the company,
And she just sleeps on the floor.
Well I know I've had it.
I don't even want to know Misery no more.

"Confronting a Corruption Within"

A hand,
  Reaches from the depths,
    Pointing imperiously at me,
      Judging mercilessly.
A room-shaking voice begins to speak.
      Speaking ill of the whole.
Well-founded opinions,
    Mistaken for fact.
Speaking more and more precisely,
     Demanding more and more precision.
The hand demands I make the decision,
    To see that darkness
Is not a blanket,
   But a patchwork of small dark energies.
      However, porous,
For without light,
   The perceptual abyss,
     Would just be emptiness.
"The shadows are founded on equality"
     It tells me.
A flash of light broke the lecture,
    And the omniscient hand vanished.
I wondered,
   If truth brought this voice of such reason,
     What force of light,
      Drove it away?
Which one here is purity?
   If either at all?
  Or was this all the work of one,
   Where this was just a demonstration of equality?

Wasting my time
enjoying myself
staring at the clouds chaser
watching as everyword
I write
falls off
the
page

I've been lost
            For so long,
                        But I was found!
        In the elation of vibrations.
                                A mental voyage vacation.
        Through frequencies,
                    And God-tasting.
                                Not a moment worth wasting.
                        For I am facing:
        Those whose souls
                    Make my heart chase.
                        For we occupy the same space,
                                But our race is of another place!
I know I may sound crazed,
            And the look on your face tells me
                        You'll be asking your girlfriends
                            To let you borrow their mace,
                                    "Just in case."
But I'm harmless,
            Maybe a bit too honest,
                        But I'm on it.
                            Cause you don't know when I started.
But let's get to the show,
            Cause I don't want you acting like
                        You've got to go…
                                So…I am here to,
                                        Try to,
Bridge your minds, and in due time,
            We will all be one soul combined.
                            Just passion in disguise.
Ready to,

Be let loose,
                Ready to explode!
And open up a hole,
            In your chest.
                    Creating a conduit,
                            To the collective consciousness.
Filling in the shrunken raisin grooves of your brain…
        See! I told you this dude's insane,
                            And here he brings it up again!
            At least that's for all that they can complain…
        So to leave you on a saner note,
                    Here's a limerick a ghost wrote:
Sometimes I wish I had less to say,
        But I know that change is on its way,
                    So believe the myth:
                            Truth still exists.
            For even Rome didn't corrupt in a day.

This is <u>The Epilogue of "Free Spirit."</u>
                    The poison still runs through
                              The veins of the herd.
We as honest animals,
            Should see such betrayal,
                        As nothing less than absurd.

Those who listened in the past,
                    Should now be deafened by the silence.
It seems we've become accustomed,
                    While awakened by the science.

Lines of people in escape,
                    This fate we cannot change,
For Mother Earth,
        Who gave us birth,
                    Has now become estranged,
And Father Sky looks upon us ashamed,
                    In a rage.
                        For what we see,
                            As reality,
                                Is a stage.
I cannot say this is the end,
            As naively we believe it so.
                    Everything's in revolution
                            This era we must let go.
A new circle will start,
            And a calender begins,
                    But our existence now an oxymoron,
                            Much like a safety pin.
The serpent eats its tail,
            As the morals that keep us "safe,"
                    Were created by those secure.

They're the last strings that keep
                Our souls to our shoes,
                        For now religion's a dirty word.

In the past,
        Evil wasn't so concealed,
But as things go on,
        Darkness has found better places to hide.
Not so easily revealed,
            Hidden in every advance.
We must be conscience of
            The evil inside.

The wishes of madmen got us this far,
And there's no telling how it'll end.
There's no turning back on the same road now,
No matter how much money you spend.

The well-born,
        Instinctively content.
                No need of compensation.
                        No need of self-assurance.
                                Birthed comfortably, in a down bed.
Silver spoon in mouth, without a word said.
                Natural enemy of those lower,
                        For the fragile fear the unknown,
                                And the pedestal too high to reach.
                        No rites of passage, nor trials,
                                But still bestowed the right to preach.
Set the moral standard,
        As if you were the pure.
                You determine good, from bad, from evil,
                        As if you were so sure.
The poor look up in ignorance,
        While the well-born look down their noses.
                We drink the dirty water,
                        While the clean goes to their roses.

My Little Nietzsche
"A thinker sees his own actions as experiments and questions—as attempts to find out something. Success and failure are for him answers above all."
—Friedrich Nietzsche

The several severed signs
        On the side of the road,
Just makes me wonder
        If I was born cold,
Cause everything I had,
        Worth anything, I sold,
            Just for a taste of freedom.

The man who leans forward,
        Stands on his head.
Doesn't listen, but hears,
        Every word that's been said.
He seems to know everybody,
        But doesn't have any friends,
          Cause in the end, he's all that he's thinking.

An old man with squinting eyes,
        Talks with a slur.
He says he's lived quite a life,
        But what he remembers is a blur.
Says he's traveled the world,
        But where, he's not sure.
           I guess we both just wasted our breath.

A circle of men of gray hair
        Try to make our decisions,
They rather not help,
        But to force their opinion.
They're all shaking hands
        To avoid ever listening.
          These people have lost their purpose.

The woman in rags,

Handing out flowers,
Spends her day
Guilting people for hours,
But why give money to someone,
Who wouldn't spend some on showers?
Is her health not worth investing?

So I sit here thinking
By the side of a lake,
Maybe all of my decisions,
Have been slight mistakes,
Wondering how long it'll be,
Until someone takes my place,
Lying in my bed next to her.

The artist and his pen,
Speaks nothing but silence.
The most peaceful of men,
But his visions are of violence.
He takes our bound minds,
And forcefully unties us.
There are just so many, unwilling.

Just because something not fragile,
                        Doesn't mean it won't break.
You just need to understand,
                        How much pressure it can take.

The cracked hourglass
Has no sense of direction
Any longer.
It had misplaced its purpose
Somewhere in the chase.

The perpetual pendulum
Had lost its tempo
In the sand on the floor.
Reliving memories
It'd rather erase.

The six-sided serpent
Has slowly casted
A four.
She didn't realize
It was checkmate.

The wide winding road
Is always asking
For more.
But it is now finding it
Harder to relate.

I'm a slave to my own ambitions,
Absolutely inefficient
Bound from the inside,
Tied from behind,
What a dreary chore
That is my mind.

Mariachi and meditation.
A living contradiction.

Just a flashing vision.
A living contradiction.

Just here for the ride,
Wearing a disguise.
I take it off at times,
And watch from the side.

Darkness hidden in fire,
Your true desire.
Partial truths don't make you
Any less of a liar.

Living on the edge of thought,
I honestly forgot,
For sometimes it just isn't
What it is,
It's what it's not.

<u>Shy,</u>
Shifting eyes.
Peeking,
From the corner,
She spies.
Leering,
But appearing,
As if looking astray.
So coy.
She sneaks away.
We'll both regret this day.
No hello,
Is as good as
Goodbye.
That's what I say.

Held together
      By fragments
         Of false awakening.
Sinister contemplation
         Leads to personal damnation.
Self-adhesive thoughts,
         That are at best self-destructive,
Drifting between twilight and day,
          Repelling sleep,
            With someone so seductive.

Facts fall through the fingers,
Of those, closed-minded.
Steal the breath from the lungs,
Of those who deny it.

Sell the skin off the teeth,
Of those smiling.
And hold tight the drops,
Of those crying.

An infallible value,
For those who give it worth.
Priceless and immalleable,
For those that gave it birth.

Seems nothing human hands hold,
Stays pure on this earth.
It's time to change what we know for sure,
For the better or worse.

The Chalk Walkway

These paved pathways,
    And corroding concrete alleys,
        Seem so novel to me.
Such dissolution,
    Must have some sort of story.
Nothing is so
    Unnaturally decayed.
      Man's Midas touch
        Has such
          Rippling gravity.
The power to improve
    And depreciate.
      That can be done
      In the same,
        Subtle,
        Brushstroke.
    I stray,
      I stray,
          And I come to:
A chalk walkway
    Which leads to descending stairs,
      Where I can only assume there
        To be a bottom.
There are no flights,
    Nor railings,
      Just a spiraling staircase
        Downwards.
As I teeter on the top step,
    I slowly look down.
      My heart begins to race.
        The blood,

                                        Rushes to my face.
My ears begin to ring,
                And a strong sense of confidence
                                        Overcomes me.
I decide my next step forward…
                                …Is down.
I begin to traverse.
                With every step,
                The clicking of my heels
                                Reflects back,
                                        As if to remind me.
I feel as though,
                I am somehow progressing.
At this point,
                I've lost sight
                        Of where I've started.
Not from the stairs above,
                        But from the encroaching
                                        Shroud of darkness.
The air becomes
                Increasingly thin,
                        And it shoots
                                Chills through my skin.
I look around to see
                That I am embedded
                In the shroud,
                        But the steps around me
                                Are clearly visible, as if inviting.
I maintain a steady pace
                        Further down.
The purpose of this journey
                Seemingly slips my mind with
                        The awning of shadows overhead…

Fear now my motivation.

I feel as though the life is being
Drained from me,
Along with my
Constitution.

I never ask "why?"
But "where?":
"Where is this taking me?"
As if content with
Whatever plans it has.

With no railings,
There's nothing to keep me
From falling to the abyss below.
The acute thrill of death,
Breeds a rush of adrenaline.

With that, I speed up to
A galloping pace,
Hoping for a swifter solution.

It is almost as though
I haven't moved an inch.
My footsteps keep me company.

I build up a sweat,
And a pressure builds.
I succumb to a "watched" feeling.
I feel as though I'm being toyed with.
Like some test subject.

My chest begins to tighten.
My head starts to spin.
A flush of vertigo hits me.
I fall atop my back,
To keep from rolling off.

I seep into the sharp steps behind.
A sick relief,

And the darkened vista,
Fades to white…
The twisting stairs
Where I lie,
Seem to level out,
And meld into a fine cushion.
I'm surrounded by
Familiar voices of comfort,
Shame,
Despair…
As I crack an eye,
I notice that the chalk walkway,
The stairway, it led to,
And the shroud,
Have been replaced
By flickering flourescent lights
Overhead.
I am unable to move.
Hindered.
I feel a stinging in my chest,
But no feeling.
I am strapped down,
With an elaborate array
Of plastic veins,
Webbing out of every appendage.
I see a patch on my chest
Where the stabbing feeling was.
Still…no pain…
Have I forgotten??
Finally, a man in white
Walks to me,
And says:
"You're lucky, son"

And I realized then,
      That the shroud had spared me,
            For the chalk walkway leads only down.

      (Certainly my poem, but not my journey.)

You'll never be as cold,
As the day you see
Her name in stone.
So alone…

<u>I am a child no longer…</u>
All ignorant bliss of the past
Is long forgotten.
I have felt fate's fatal grip
Squeeze what can only be described
As a heart, until every semblance
Of emotion and will was dripped dry.
It hurt not,
Well I cannot honestly say…
I lost the definition of that word
Long before.
In the springtime, what gave birth
relented to rest.
My compatriots of summers yore were
Consumed by confusion.
The fall is a constant present.
While the winter…
Well…the winter took my love away.

Well, why am I still here to speak?
I must have somewhere to go…
Or maybe it's simply because I've yet to
Forget a thing about you.

Wasting time in,
      What could have been.
Wallowing,
      In someone else's misery.
Even in the eye,
      You're not entirely safe,
         From the surrounding storm.
As the winds of change shift,
    I sit,
      In sincerity,
        Like stone.
As the wrathful elements
    Rush and whip around me.
      Scarring my vessel in sharp judgement.
        Torturing my mind with spiraling doubt.
In silent anguish, I cope.
      Out of habit, I hope.
         Out of despair, I sigh.
     Darkness swirls around the center of the sky.
      Clouds scatter in terror.
      The stars fly to the
      Surrounding horizon.
Connecting to form a belt of glowing constellations.
      The sky blinks.
      I'm shaken,
      But I lie content,
      For there is nothing,
        These hands,
         Can do.

Words have only gotten me so far,
           And in seemingly the wrong direction.
I now reserve my judgement,
           For something more in my benefit.

What I've learned so far is that, if any one thing, happiness is the meaning of life. Therefore, you should let nothing get in the way of what makes you happy. However, it is not as if everything goes your way. So to assure that fate is in your favor, you have to release yourself to the flow of appreciation, so that with every moment that becomes "now," it is accepted and assessed in positivity.

I believe that is what is meant by "riding the flow" or "being in sync": being in the now, and making the best of every moment. This is because happiness can only be found within, but we're constantly influenced by the world we walk through. Therefore, the root of happiness is acceptance of the moment.

Fully focusing on the moment can only be achieved as a result of yoga. And to carry that mentality/mind-state into the waking, walking life, is to be closest to the flow as we can conceive it (or not). There's no need for over-speculation on the matter, just acknowledge the means to the end. The path amongst the tall grass. Also, in my experience, the more the world of the transcendental mindset and the physical world are brought to a point within, the less of a division, and less the separation from the flow. To be closer to the source of energy and creation is to be more in tune with its all-nurturing methods/vibration.

I Claw the glass cage,
So clear I can breathe through it.
Is it even there?

I want to be a raven
           On the run.
To fly freely,
           And to black out the sun.
I don't need protection,
           Nor technology.
I don't want your liberties,
           Nor security.
I want to be whole,
           As One.

For a friend I once claimed, I didn't know.
...How do you not realize what lies down that road?

These thoughts linger
On the tip of my tongue,
Like the last drop of blood
From the syringe.

You've always been
My strong-willed brother,
But I sense that
Something's unhinged.

I see the reflection of
Someone forgotten,
In the puddle those drops
Left on the floor.

And it's that lingering
Thirst for life,
That has left you out
Craving for more.

<u>My black jeans</u>
        Are now faded gray,
            From the sun,
                  And the winds I've faced.
The heels are tattered,
        From sidewalks stumbled over.
             The holes in the back pockets,
                     From rest.
There are tears in the knees,
        From the world weighing me down.
                Bringin' me down…
                  Draggin' me around.
The rip near my thigh,
        Is from a fight,
             On a night I can't honestly remember.
The bleach stain on my lap
        Is to remind me, how I've changed.
                Oh, how I've changed!
          Been estranged, rearranged.
And the white paint on the
        Back of my knee, is from
            The world I wish to create,
               In contrast of the darkness I've seen.
They may not be my only pair,
        Or the cleanest thing I wear,
             But they fit me like
                They were always there.

Figments of a Fight

A swollen face
Encased in towers,
Slowly weakening
With the constant onslaught.

The bright lights overhead
Dim, then turn
From blue to red.

A blur of rage,
And the pound
Of a drum
Beats from within.

The smell of blood
Overcomes all senses.
The ground shakes
With the bloom of a roar.

The towers become
Increasingly
Shadowed.

The lights
Now flicker.

A bell goes off,
And there's a pull.
Things become cleaner.
The towers fall.

I'm left in a haze of
Vague voices
Of comfort,
And encouragement.

"Stay in there!"
The only clear call
As the bell goes off
Once again.

I feel a push,
And the towers are
Erected once more.

The drum starts up,
Slow, until it
Settles in tempo.

…It ends,
In a pop…

And everything stops…

Turns from red,
To black.
Followed by a wave
Of white relief.

A face appears,
And whispers:
"Not yet."

Flashes startle me,

As things appear
More familiar.

A voice calls out:
"Seven…eight…nine…ten!"
And that
Friendly bell rings again.
With that call,
I know now,
These towers will rise no more

I did not awake,
        Something deep inside
                Dilated.
           Opening up a new understanding,
      A grasp of the vibrations.
A connection with all around,
           Aware or not.
A swinging mantra
      That floats upwards and outwards,
                        Around and inwards.
           Perpetually churning
  Like some varying constant.
           Always there, though not always in tune.
An innate language,
        That rusts,
           At the speed of remembrance.
Practice breeds naturality,
        As many a teacher of
           Language has told me.
And no matter how learned,
           Knowledge drifts away with time.
However,
    All becomes second nature,
           Once you forget
              It's foreign.
I cannot specifically say how so,
           For I'm one and the same,
                Still searching.
    And you can be sure,
        That even in the end,
           You are never done learning.
There is no other way,
        To say,

That this is just the game
Of realization,
We play.

Thy blood runs blue,
        Icy like a crystal river.
When exposed,
      It will show you,
           Only that which you want to see.

Surely, things are not as they appear.
         Obviously disguised,
            As if on masquerade.
A constant curtain of illusion,
        As tactile and prideful as a crusade.

Broken down on unachieved goals,
        And failed initiatives,
          That must have some gravity.
As much as it seems so trivial
        Others can only lay claim,
           To what you have seen.

Thy true-self,
      Puts thy life in a fish eye.
           Sets thy world into frame.
It tells thee thine art the only creatures on Earth
        To devalue love,
         And honor fame.

Letting fate lead the way,
For I'm afraid of nothing.
Even in this darkened hour,
I know good things are coming.

They say that things get better,
Right before the storm.
Well now I'm in the midst of it,
As it guides me to the shore.

I take your words as truth.
We held tight each other's hands.
Walking along the shore,
With our feet planted in the sand.

We were soon uprooted
Forced to go our own ways
However, the memory of your touch,
Retains the feeling of those days.

When the sky starts
                    Crumbling down around you,
                              A person tends to
                                        Put up walls.
Some life-changing situations,
                    Can often be too much for anyone.
It allows your brain to start firing off
                    All these random impulses and emotions,
                              Void of logic.
All thoughts hastily speeding by,
                    Forgetting it takes time to hold on.
They feel so important,
                    And no matter how trivial,
                              It's just far too much at once.
I know I'm not alone when I say:
                    A person tends to shut down.
I'm not talking about grief,
                    I'm talking about pressure…
I'm talking about all of your friends,
                    Family,
                    Your girl,
                              Your apartment,
                                        Car,
                                        And bills,
On the second floor of a two-story brownstone lined with
                    Photos of people of importance,
                              Encased in elaborate gold frames,
          And you're stuck in the basement,
                    As the support beams snap inwards.
You're there, with your arms to the ceiling,
          Desperately gasping for air
                    Between muscle spasms
                    From trying to keep everything you know

                    Above your head.

This is where…
            I give up.
                I let that shitty, decaying house,
                            Crash upon me.
And every time it does,
                    And oh it does…
I pray I will somehow
                Piece together
                    My remains,
                        And become a stronger man,
However, I come out the same person,
                With a better understanding,
                            And a stronger foundation.
All the fragile crystalline luxuries
                Such as faith, trust, and hope,
                            Shatter in the chaos.
I am left alone,
            Trying to rebuild the walls of my only home
                    Every time the sky comes crashing down.

_____

I feel when I was younger,
        I saw through different eyes.
Sometimes now, I can catch the same
        Spirits in the corner of my sight.
They come to me in visions,
        In the hollow of the night.
Where I squint, and somewhat see,
        The way I did, earlier in life.

Is your heart as light
        As a feather?
How well have you kept
        Yourself together?
Have you shown gratitude
        For what's been given?
How far along are you
        In your mission?
Have the people who've hurt you
        Been forgiven?
How much living have you
        Done living?

Take the tools you're given,
        And reuse them.
Take what you've learned,
        And teach.
Take what you know,
        And preach.
Taste your fears,
        And see what's at stake.
Live your life,
     Don't hesitate!
For excuses are those
        That hinder fate.

I put sage in my cigarettes.
                    Watch the aura burn.
Etherical influence
                    Sets in,
                              And expresses its sympathy in smoke.
Otherworldly avatars,
                    Agitated
                              By forced entry.
My abode,
          Ever-changing since infancy.
The bright light
          From behind the door,
                    Clouded by years of conditioning.
Though unlocked,
          The door is blocked by piles
                              Of preconceptions.
I try to always leave
          A window cracked
                    For the light to shine through,
                              But the spirits appreciate
                                        Entering with the least burden.
I've spent years
          Shifting and sorting
                    The mess of my domain.
I've come to the conclusion:
                    I'm better off with nothing,
                              Or close to it.
So I can maintain what I add,
                    And keep.
Instead of the burden of nostalgia,
                    And the torment,
                              Of parting piece by piece.
With a cleared floor,

I know for sure,
                    I can always easily open the door.
            And the light will
                    Never again have trouble entering.
The spirits,
        Grateful,
                Will not hesitate in their blessings.
                We should have boundless respect for the unknown.

The air
Is filled
With dreams
And Prana.
There is no empty space,
Only vague perceptions.
Blindfolded
In a sea
Of congealed
Energies.
In the midst of the void,
This void of existence.
Are many shades
Of birth and death.
The time and space allotted
To feel,
Breathe,
Act.
All that's left, when you go
Is your weight.
And your job in life,
Is to be conscious of your footprint.

Reality,
    But a thought,
        Willed into existence
            By infinite forces
                Of polar nature.
The exhale of Source,
    Expansively breathing life
        Into the perceptual nothingness of space.
Life brewing
    around light.
Nothing created without purpose,
        Emotion.
     Emotion, the fuel of will.
     Will, a reflection of light.
     Light, the foundation of emptiness.
Without the understanding of light,
        There is no framework for darkness.
This is the basis of
    Nature's flow
        Of equilibrium.
There is no creation or destruction.
        It is an illusion of Maya,
            Of duality.
There is only the manifest and
        Unmanifest of matter.
            Use and reuse.
Everything is birthed,
    Disassembled,
      And rebirthed.
    All that is given life, eventually has it taken.
But nothing is ever lost.
      Nothing is lost…
        Not a drop left behind…

Every wondrous miracle, molecule,
                    Was so at a cost.
It's not as clear to sight,
            As black to white.
                    But you can certainly
                            Tell a balance.
As Shiva
        Displays the divine dance
                    Of recreation.
It paves the way,
            For Brahma
                To re-breed
                        Karmic creation.
            To reinstate the divine vibration.
It is just the way:
            Dharmatic unification.

Half-eyed within the
Divine. Flawed vessel, nothing,
To the polished mind.

The Earth, our mother,
Is going to sing.
Oh,
What a loving change
It will bring.
Her hum to a roar,
What a perfect pitch!
It'll crack open the ears
Of those who have never heard
True music.
Sound you can love.
Frequencies that evoke
Such profound passion.
Meditative bliss
In the form
Of auditory influence.
May we be relearning to listen?
Are we starting to play along?
Trying to hear with what we are?
Are monks musicians?
Isolated up in the hills striving to
Get an ear to the monitor?
Hoping to get that perfect,
Everlasting track,
By first finding a place
Clear of feedback.
Trying…trying…
To have a conversation.
Only comprehended,
Not listened to.
To finally have that call,
Free of static
And disturbance.

Whenever you
        Call someone you love,
                And there's interference,
      Where they're just not coming in completely clear,
It can be tolerated for a while...
            But...it eats at you.
You might not
          Even realize it,
             But eventually,
                  It goes beyond annoyance.
Bothered to the point
        of breaking.
           They're saying:
      "Come on! Please, could ya...
  Could ya please...just clear up that little bit of static!?
          Maybe get a new phone for once!?
Cause it's just...it's just....you know...
       ...A little too much after a while!
           Can't you hear that!? It's not hard to fix!"
And they're right,
      It's only natural.
            Our skies are cloudy,
                 Not the heavens.
Also, Gaia is always firm
        Beneath our feet.
In fact, her song is
      Always sung.
         In the end, that's probably
               How it all begun.
In a hum,
   A vibration,
      From source,
         To soul.

And it's that "Oooooooooooooom,"
That affirms,
This is our home.

Oh! Let Gaia's ring
Play eternal!
Let it wash over
Unbaptized ears.
Splitting us open,
Exposing the Earth to ourselves.
May she answer your inquiries,
Your pleas.
May you reestablish peace,
Be aware of your fellow leaves,
Praise the life-giving tree,
Our only planet,
Our home.